Marx in Soho

Howard Zinn

Marx in Soho

A Play on History

Haymarket Books
Chicago, IL

© 1999 by Howard Zinn

First published in 1999 by South End Press.
This edition published in 2013 by Haymarket Books.
P.O. Box 180165
Chicago, IL 60618
773-583-7884
info@haymarketbooks.org
www.haymarketbooks.org

ISBN: 978-1-60846-301-5

Trade distribution:
In the U.S. through Consortium Book Sales and Distribution, www.
cbsd.com
In the UK, Turnaround Publisher Services, www.turnaround-uk.com
In Canada, Publishers Group Canada, www.pgcbooks.ca
In Australia, Palgrave Macmillan, www.palgravemacmillan.com.au
All other countries, Publishers Group Worldwide, www.pgw.com

Special discounts are available for bulk purchases by organizations
and institutions. Please contact Haymarket Books for more information
at 773-583-7884 or info@haymarketbooks.org.

This book was published with the generous support of
the Wallace Global Fund and Lannan Foundation.

Printed in the United States by union labor.

Library of Congress CIP Data is available.

1 3 5 7 9 10 8 6 4 2

table of
contents

f●rew●rd

I first read the *Communist Manifesto* — given to me, I am sure, by young Communists who lived in my working-class neighborhood — when I was about seventeen. It had a profound effect on me, because everything I saw in my own life, the life of my parents, and the conditions in the United States in 1939 seemed to be explained, put into a historical context, and placed under a powerful analytical light.

I could see that my father, a Jewish immigrant from Austria, with but a fourth-grade education, worked very very hard, yet could barely support his wife and four sons. I could see that my mother worked day and night to make sure we were fed, clothed, and taken care of when we were sick. Their lives were an unending struggle for survival. I knew too that there were people in the nation who possessed astonishing wealth, and who certainly did not work as hard as my parents. The system was not fair.

All around me in that time of depression were families in desperate need through no fault of their own; unable to pay the rent, their belongings were thrown out on the street by the landlord, backed by the law. I knew from the newspapers that this was true all over the country.

I was a reader. I had read many of Dickens' novels since I was thirteen, and they had awakened within me an indignation against injustice, a compassion for people treated cruelly by their employers, by the legal system. Now, in 1939, I read John Steinbeck's *The Grapes of Wrath,* and that indignation returned, this time directed at the rich and powerful in this country.

In the *Manifesto*, Marx and Engels (Marx was thirty, Engels twenty-eight, and Engels said later that Marx was the principal writer) described what I was experiencing, what I was reading about, which, I now saw, was not an aberration of nineteenth-century England or depression-era America, but a fundamental truth about the capitalist system. And this system, deeply entrenched as it was in the modern world, was not eternal —

it had come into being at a certain stage of history, and one day it would depart the scene, replaced by a socialist system. That was an inspiring thought.

"The history of all hitherto existing society is the history of class struggles," they proclaimed in the opening pages of the *Manifesto*. So, the rich and the poor did not face each other as individuals, but as classes. This made the conflict between them something monumental. And it suggested that working people, poor people, had something to bind them together in their quest for justice — their common membership in the working class.

And what of the role of the government in that struggle of the classes? "Equal justice for all" was carved on the facade of public buildings. But in the *Manifesto*, Marx and Engels wrote: "The executive of the modern state is but a committee for managing the common affairs of the whole bourgeoisie." They presented a startling idea: that the machinery of government was not neutral, that, despite its pretensions, it served the capitalist class.

At the age of seventeen, I suddenly saw this idea dramatized. My Communist friends brought me along with them to a demonstration in Times Square. Hundreds of people unfurled banners proclaiming opposition to war, opposition to Fascism, and marched along the street. I heard sirens. Mounted police charged the crowd. I was knocked unconscious by a plainclothes policeman. When I came to, as my head was clearing, I could only think one troubling thought: the police, the state, did the bidding of the holders of great wealth. How much freedom of speech and freedom of assembly you had depended on what class you were in.

When, at the age of eighteen, I went to work in a shipyard in Brooklyn as an apprentice shipfitter (our job was to fit together, with rivets, with welding, the steel plates of the hulls of battleships), I was already "class-conscious." In the shipyard, I found three other young workers like myself, and the four of us undertook to organize our fellow apprentices, who were excluded from the craft unions. We also agreed to meet weekly and read the works of Marx and Engels.

Thus I read Engels' exposition of Marxist philosophy in his book *Anti-Dühring* (a polemic against a writer named Dühring) and made my way laboriously through the first volume of *Das Kapital*. The system, I saw, with some excitement, was now laid bare. Behind all the complications of economic transactions, there were certain core truths: labor was the source of all value; labor produced a value beyond its meager wages; and that surplus value went into the pockets of the capitalist class. Capitalists needed unemployment — a "reserve army of labor" — to keep wages down. The system cherished things, especially money, more than people ("commodity fetishism"), so that everything good in life was measured by its exchange value.

Marxist theory explained that exploitation and class struggle were not new phenomena in world history, but that capitalism brought them to their sharpest point, and on a world scale. Capitalism was a progressive force in history at a certain stage of human development. "The bourgeoisie, historically, has played a most revolutionary part," they wrote in the *Manifesto*. It has enabled enormous technological and scientific progress, created huge wealth. But this became concentrated in fewer and fewer hands. There was a fundamental conflict between the increasingly organized forces of production and the anarchy of the market system. At some point, the exploited proletariat would organize, rebel, take power, and use the advanced technology for human need, not for the enrichment of the capitalist class.

That was my early introduction to Marx. Years later — after serving as a bombardier in the Eighth Air Force in World War II and going to college and graduate school with the help of the G.I. Bill of Rights and the support of my wife and two children — I began to teach history and politics, first in the South at Spelman College. After seven years at Spelman, I accepted a job at Boston University and moved north. In my courses in political theory, I paid serious attention to the writings of Marx and Engels.

At some point in the late 1960s, I became interested in anarchism, for several reasons. One was the growing evidence of the horrors of Stalinism in the Soviet Union, which suggested that the classical Marxian concept of "the dictatorship of the proletariat" needed to be reconsidered. Another was my own experience in the South in the struggle against racial segregation spearheaded by the Student Nonviolent Coordinating Committee. SNCC (Snick, as it was called), without any self-conscious theorizing, acted in accord with anarchist principles: no central authority, grassroots democratic decision-making. In the New Left of the 1960s, this was called "participatory democracy."

I began to read about anarchism, beginning with the American anarchist-feminist Emma Goldman and her friend Alexander Berkman. I went on to Peter Kropotkin and Mikhail Bakunin. Bakunin was a fierce opponent of Marx's concept of how a revolution should come about. Emma Goldman, deported to Russia from the United States in 1919 for opposing World War I, observed that the new Soviet state was imprisoning not just its bourgeois opponents but dissident revolutionaries, and harshly criticized what she considered a betrayal of the socialist dream. This immersion in anarchist thought led me to initiate a seminar at Boston University on "Marxism and Anarchism."

From 1965 (the year of serious escalation of the war in Vietnam) to 1975 (when the Saigon government surrendered), I was heavily involved in the movement against the war, and my writings were very much concentrated on issues connected with the war. When the war ended, I felt free to do other things, and I wrote a play about Emma Goldman, *Emma,* which was performed in Boston and New

York, and years later in London and Tokyo. In one of the play's scenes, young New York revolutionaries in a Lower East Side café argue about Marx's ideas versus Bakunin's.

I was very interested in the personal lives of these thinkers. Emma Goldman's autobiography, *Living My Life*, was a candid account of her tempestuous life as a rebel, not only in politics, but in sex. Marx never wrote an autobiography, but I could turn to a number of biographies for insights into his private life. In addition, there was a brilliant biography of his daughter Eleanor Marx by the English writer Yvonne Kapp, in which she recounts the details of the Marx family's life in London.

Karl and Jenny Marx had moved to London after he was expelled from country after country on the European continent. They lived in the grubby Soho district, and revolutionaries from all over Europe, arriving in London, trooped in and out of their home. That imagined scene — Marx at home, Marx with his wife, Jenny, with his daughter Eleanor — fascinated me.

My happy experience with the Emma Goldman play had lured me into the world of the theater, and I set out to write a play about Karl Marx. I wanted

foreword

to show Marx as few people knew him, as a family man, struggling to support his wife and children. Three of the children had died very early, and three daughters survived.

I also wanted the audience to see Marx defending his ideas against attack. I knew his wife, Jenny, was a formidable thinker herself, and I imagined her confronting Marx from time to time. I knew that his daughter Eleanor was a precociously brilliant child, and I could see her challenging some of his most sophisticated theories. I wanted to subject Marx's ideas to an anarchist critique, and decided to invent a visit to his home by Bakunin. (In fact, there is no record of such a visit, although Marx and Bakunin knew one another and were fierce opponents inside the International Workingmen's Association, the First International.)

There was something else I thought missing from usual appraisals of Marx. The emphasis was always on Marx the thinker, the theoretician. I knew that Marx was extraordinarily active as a revolutionary, first as a rebellious journalist in Germany, then with workers' associations in Paris and the Communist League in Brussels. He was active in the Rhineland during the European revolutions of 1848, which led to his trial and acquittal after a dramatic speech in court. After his exile to London, he was involved with the International Workingmen's Association, with the cause of Irish freedom, and in 1871 as a supporter of the Paris Commune.

His writings during these years were not only theoretical writings in political economy, as in *Das Kapital*, but immediate reactions to political events, to the 1848 revolutions, to the Commune of Paris, to workers' struggles all over the continent. I therefore wanted to put on stage this other side of Marx — the passionate, engaged revolutionary. The play I wrote included as characters Marx, his wife, Jenny, his daughter Eleanor, his friend Engels, and his political rival Bakunin. It had a reading in Boston that was well received, but which didn't satisfy me. I then set out to turn it into a one-person play.

My wife, Roslyn, always a perceptive critic of my writing, kept prodding me to make the play more directly relevant to our time, rather than a historical piece about Marx and Europe in the nineteenth century. I knew she was right about this, and, after wrestling with it for a while, came up with the idea that Marx, in a kind of fantasy, would return from wherever he was to the present. Furthermore, he would return to the United States, so that he could not only reminisce about his life in nineteenth-century Europe, but comment on what is happening here today. I decided I would have the authorities, whoever they are, return him, by bureaucratic error, not to Soho in London where he lived, but to Soho in New York.

Although it was a one-person play, I would have Marx bring to life, through his reminiscences, the important people in his life, especially his wife, Jenny, and his daughter Eleanor. And he would bring back Bakunin, the anarchist. All of them, in different ways, would be subjecting Marx's ideas to blunt criticism. There would be a dialectic of opposing viewpoints, presented through Marx's own recapturing of the arguments.

I wrote the play at a time when the collapse of the Soviet Union brought an almost universal exultation in the mainstream press and among political leaders: not only was "the enemy" gone, but the ideas of Marxism were discredited. Capitalism and the "free market" had triumphed. Marxism had failed. Marx was truly dead. I thought it important, therefore, to make it clear that neither the Soviet

Union, nor other countries that called themselves "Marxist" but had set up police states, represented Marx's notion of socialism. I wanted to show Marx as angry that his theories had been so distorted as to stand for Stalinist cruelties. I thought it necessary to rescue Marx not only from those pseudo-socialists who established repressive rule in various parts of the world, but also from all those writers and politicians in the West who now gloated over the triumph of capitalism.

Marx's critique of capitalism, I wanted to show, remains fundamentally true in our time. His analysis is corroborated every day in the newspaper headlines. He saw the unprecedented speed and chaos of technological change and social change in his time, which is even more true today. "Constant revolutionizing of production, uninterrupted disturbance of all social conditions, everlasting uncertainty and agitation distinguish the bourgeois epoch from all earlier ones. All fixed, fast-frozen relations, with their train of ancient and venerable prejudices and opinions, are swept away, all new-formed ones become antiquated before they can ossify. All that is solid melts into air." This was in the *Manifesto*.

foreword

What we speak of as "globalization" Marx saw very clearly. Again, the *Manifesto*: "The need of a constantly expanding market for its products chases the bourgeoisie over the whole surface of the globe. It must nestle everywhere, settle everywhere, establish connections everywhere. . . . In place of the old local and national seclusion and self-sufficiency, we have intercourse in every direction, universal interdependence of nations." The "free-trade agreements" sought by the United States government in recent years are attempts to remove whatever restrictions there are to the free flow of capital across the globe — giving capitalists the right to exploit people everywhere.

The headlines Marx looks at in the course of the play are not surprising to him. He saw the mergers of huge enterprises, which go on today, but on a larger scale. He saw the growing gap between the rich and the poor, which is true not just within each country but, even more dramatically, between the people of rich nations and those of poor nations.

In the play, Marx says that socialism should not take on the characteristics of capitalism. Observing how opponents of the regime have been put to death in pseudo-socialist countries, he reflects on what he said about the system of crime and punishment when he was writing in the *New York Daily Tribune* in 1853: "Is there not a necessity for deeply reflecting upon the alteration of the system that breeds these crimes, instead of glorifying the hangman who executes a lot of criminals to make room only for the supply of new ones?"

We live in a society that Marx's phrase "commodity fetishism" perfectly describes. As Ralph Waldo Emerson put it, roughly around the same time, watching the beginning of the American industrial system: "Things are in the saddle and ride mankind." The protection of corporate property is deemed more important than the protection of human life. Indeed, the Supreme Court decided in the late nineteenth century that a corporation was "a person" and so protected by the Fourteenth Amendment, more protected, in fact, than black people, for whom that amendment was originally written.

Marx was but twenty-five years old, living in Paris with Jenny, when he wrote a remarkable document, published only many years later, known as *The Economic and Philosophical Manuscripts*. Marx wrote there about alienation in the modern world, brought to its peak under capitalism, with human beings alienated from their labor, from nature, from one another, and from their own true selves. This is a phenomenon we see all around us in our time, one that results in psychological as well as material misery.

Marx devoted most of his writing to a critique of capitalism and very little to a description of what a socialist society might look like. But we can extrapolate from what he says about capitalism to imagine a society without exploitation, where people feel at one with nature, with the work they do, with each other, and with themselves. Marx gives us some clues about the future when he describes in glowing terms the society created by the Paris Commune of 1871 in the few short months of its existence. I tried to incorporate that vision in this play.

Those who read *Marx in Soho* may wonder how much is historically accurate. The major events in Marx's life and in the history of the era are fundamentally true: his marriage to Jenny, his exile to London, the death of his three children, and the political conflicts of the time: the Irish struggle against England, the 1848 revolutions in Europe, the Communist movement, the Paris Commune. The main characters he talks about are real: the members of his family, his friend Engels, his rival Bakunin. The dialogue is invented, but I have tried to be true to the personalities and the thinking of the characters, though I may be taking some liberties in imagining his ideological conflicts with Jenny and Eleanor. On a few occasions, as in his description of Napoleon III, I use Marx's own words.

My hope is that *Marx in Soho* illuminates not just that time, and Marx's place in it, but our time, and our place in it.

marx in soho

House lights up part of the way. Light on center stage, showing a bare stage, except for a table and several chairs. Marx enters, wearing a black frock coat and vest, white shirt, black floppy tie. He is bearded, short, stocky, with a black mustache and hair turning gray, wearing steel-rimmed spectacles. He is carrying a draw-sack, stops, walks to the edge of the stage, looks out at the audience, and seems pleased, a little surprised.

Thank God, an audience!

He unloads his supplies from the draw-sack: a few books, newspapers, a bottle of beer, a glass. He turns and walks to the front of the stage.

Good of you to come. You weren't put off by all those idiots who said: "Marx is dead!" Well, I am . . . and I am not. That's dialectics for you.

He doesn't mind joking about himself or his ideas. Perhaps he's mellowed over all these years. But just when you think Marx has grown soft, there are bursts of anger.

1

You may wonder how I got here . . . *smiles mischievously* . . . public transportation.

His accent is slightly British, slightly continental, nothing to draw attention, but definitely not American.

I did not expect to come back *here* . . . I wanted to return to Soho. That's where I lived in London. But . . . a bureaucratic mix-up. Here I am, Soho in New York . . . *Sighs.* Well, I always wanted to visit New York. *Pours himself some beer, takes a drink, puts it down.*

His mood changes.

Why have I returned?

He shows a little anger.

To clear my name!

He lets that sink in.

I've been reading your newspapers . . . *Picks up a newspaper.* They are all proclaiming that my ideas are dead! It's nothing new. These clowns have been saying this for more than a hundred years. Don't you wonder: why is it necessary to declare me dead again and again?

Well, I have had it up to here. I asked for the right to come back, just for a while. But there are rules. I told you: it's a bureaucracy. It is permissible to read, even to watch. But not to travel. I protested,

2

of course. And had some support . . . Socrates told them: "The untraveled life is not worth living!" Gandhi fasted. Mother Jones threatened to picket. Mark Twain came to my defense, in his own strange way. Buddha chanted: Ommmm! But the others kept quiet. My God, at this point, what do they have to lose?

Yes, there too I have a reputation as a trouble-maker. And even there, protest works! Finally, they said, "All right, you can go. You can have an hour or so to speak your mind. But remember, *no agitating!*" They do believe in freedom of speech . . . but within limits . . . *Smiles.* They are liberals.

You can spread the word: Marx is back! For a short while. But understand one thing — I'm not a Marxist. *Laughs.* I said that once to Pieper and he almost croaked. I should tell you about Pieper. *Takes a drink of beer.*

We were living in London. Jenny and I and the little ones. Plus two dogs, three cats, and two birds. Barely living. A flat on Dean Street, near where they dumped the city's sewage. We were in London because I had been expelled from the continent. Expelled from the Rhineland, yes, from my birthplace.

3

I had done dangerous things. I was editor of a newspaper, *Der Rheinische Zeitung*. Hardly revolutionary. But I suppose the most revolutionary act one can engage in is . . . to tell the truth.

In the Rhineland, the police were arresting poor people for gathering firewood from the estates of the rich. I wrote an editorial protesting that. Then they tried to censor our paper. I wrote an editorial declaring that there was no freedom of the press in Germany. They decided to prove me right. They shut us down. Only then did we become radical — isn't that the way it is? Our last issue of the *Zeitung* had a huge headline in red ink: "Revolt!" . . . That annoyed the authorities. They ordered me out of the Rhineland.

So, I went to Paris. Where else do exiles go? Where else can you sit all night in a café and tell lies about how revolutionary you were in the old country? . . . Yes, if you are going to be an exile, be one in Paris.

Paris was our honeymoon. Jenny found a tiny flat in the Latin Quarter. Heavenly months. But the word was out, from the German police to the Paris police. It seems that the police develop an internationalist consciousness long before the workers . . .

So, I was expelled from Paris, too. We went to Belgium. Expelled again.

We came to London, where refugees come from all over the world. The English are admirable in their tolerance . . . and insufferable in their boasting about it.

He coughs, which he will do from time to time. Shakes his head.

The doctors told me the cough would go away in a few weeks. That was in 1858.

But I was telling you about Pieper. You see, in London, the political refugees from the continent marched in and out of our house. Pieper was one of them. He buzzed around me like a hornet. He was a flatterer, a sycophant. He would station himself six inches from me, to make sure I could not evade him, and he would quote from my writings. I would say: "Pieper, please don't quote me to myself."

He had the audacity to say, thinking I would be pleased, that he would translate *Das Kapital* into English. Ha! The man could not speak an English sentence without butchering it. English is a beautiful language. It is Shakespeare's language. If Shakespeare had heard Pieper speak one sentence of English, he would have taken poison!

5

But Jenny felt sorry for him. She liked to invite him to our family dinners. One evening, Pieper came and announced the formation of "The Marxist Society of London."

"A Marxist society?" I asked. "What's that?"

"We meet every week to discuss another of your writings. We read aloud, examine sentence by sentence. That's why we call ourselves Marxists — we believe completely and wholeheartedly in everything you have written."

"Completely and wholeheartedly?" I asked.

"Yes, and we would be honored, Herr Doktor Marx" — he always called me Herr Doktor Marx — "if you would address the next meeting of the Marxist society."

"I cannot do that."

"Why?" he asked.

"Because *I am not a Marxist.*" *Laughs heartily.*

I didn't mind his bad English. Mine was not that perfect. It was his way of thinking. He was an embarrassment, a satellite encircling my words, reflecting them to the world but distorting them. And then he defended the distortions like a fanatic, denouncing anyone who interpreted them differently.

I once said to Jenny: "Do you know what I fear most?"

And she said: "That the workers' revolution will never come?"

"No, that the revolution *will* come, and it will be taken over by men like Pieper — flatterers when out of power, bullies and braggarts when holding power. Dogmatists. They will speak for the proletariat and they will interpret my ideas for the world. They will organize a new priesthood, a new hierarchy, with excommunications and indexes, inquisitions and firing squads.

"All this will be done in the name of Communism, delaying for a hundred years the Communism of freedom, dividing the world between capitalist empires and Communist empires. They will muck up our beautiful dream and it will take another revolution, maybe two or three, to clean it up. That's what I fear."

No, I wasn't going to have Pieper translate *Das Kapital* into English. It represented fifteen years of work — in the conditions of Soho. Walking every morning past beggars sleeping amidst the sewage, making my way to the British Museum and its magnificent library, working there until dusk, reading,

7

reading . . . Is there anything more dull than reading political economy? *He thinks.* Yes, writing political economy.

Then, home through the darkening streets, listening to the vendors calling out the prices of their wares, and the veterans of the Crimean War, some blind, others without legs, begging for a penny in the noxious air . . . The poor-smell of London, yes.

My critics, trying to minimize what went into *Das Kapital*, would say, as they always say about radical writers, "Oh, he must have had some dreadful personal experience." Yes, if you want to make much of it, that walk home through Soho fueled the anger that went into *Das Kapital*.

I hear you saying, "Well, of course, that's how it was *then*, a century ago." Only *then?* On my way here today, I walked through the streets of your city, surrounded by garbage, breathing foul air, past the bodies of men and women sleeping on the street, huddled against the cold. Instead of a lassie singing a ballad, I heard a voice in my ear . . . *plaintively:* "Some change, sir, for a cup of coffee?"

Angry now: You call this progress, because you have motor cars and telephones and flying machines and a thousand potions to make you smell better? And people sleeping on the streets?

He picks up a newspaper and peers at it. An official report: the United States' Gross National Product (yes, gross!) last year was seven thousand billion dollars. Most impressive. But tell me, where is it? Who is profiting from it? Who is not? *Reads from the newspaper again.* Less than 500 individuals control two thousand billion dollars in business assets. Are these people more noble, more hard-working, more valuable to society than the mother in the tenement, nurturing three children through the winter, with no money to pay the heating bill?

Did I not say, a hundred and fifty years ago, that capitalism would enormously increase the wealth of society, but that this wealth would be concentrated in fewer and fewer hands? *Reads from newspaper:* "Giant merger of Chemical Bank and Chase Manhattan Bank. Twelve thousand workers will lose jobs . . . Stocks rise." And they say my ideas are dead!

Do you know Oliver Goldsmith's poem "The Deserted Village"?

Recites: "Ill fares the land to hastening ills a prey/ Where wealth accumulates and men decay." Yes, *decay.* That's what I saw as I walked through your city this morning. Houses decaying, schools decaying, human beings decaying. But then I walked a bit farther, and I was suddenly surrounded by men of obvious wealth, women in jewels and furs. Suddenly I heard the sound of sirens. Was violence being done somewhere nearby? Was a crime being committed? Was someone trying to take part of the Gross National Product, illegally, from those who had stolen it legally?

Ah, the wonders of the market system! Human beings reduced to commodities, their lives controlled by the super-commodity, money.

Lights flash threateningly. Marx looks up, confides to audience: The committee doesn't like that!

His tone softens, reminiscing. In that little flat in Soho, Jenny made hot soup and boiled potatoes. There was fresh bread from our friend the baker down the street. We would sit around the table and eat and talk about events of the day — the Irish struggle for freedom, the latest war, the stupidity of the country's leaders, a political opposition confining itself to pips and squeaks, the cowardly press . . . I suppose things are different these days, eh?

After dinner, we would clear the table and I would work. With my cigars handy, and a glass of beer. Yes, work until three or four in the morning. My books piled up on one side, the parliamentary reports piled up on another. Jenny would be at the other end of the table, transcribing — my handwriting was impossible, and she would rewrite every word of mine — can you imagine a more heroic act?

Occasionally, a crisis. No, not a world crisis. A book would be missing. One day I could not find my Ricardo. I asked Jenny: "Where is my Ricardo?"

"You mean *Principles of Political Economy?*" Well, she thought I was finished with it and she had taken it to the pawnshop.

I lost my temper. "My Ricardo! You pawned my Ricardo!"

She said: "Be quiet! Last week didn't we pawn the ring my mother gave me?"

That's how it was. *Sighs.* We pawned everything. Especially gifts from Jenny's family. When we ran out of those gifts, we pawned our clothes. One winter — do you know the London winters? — I did without my overcoat. Another time, I walked out of the house and my feet began to freeze on the snow, and then I realized: I was not wearing shoes. We had pawned them the day before.

When *Das Kapital* was published, we celebrated, but Engels had to give us some money so we could go to the pawnshop and retrieve our linens and dishes for the dinner. Engels . . . a saint. There's no other word for him. When they cut off our water, our gas, and the house was dark, our spirits low, Engels paid the bills. His father owned factories in Manchester. Yes . . . *smiling* . . . capitalism saved us!

He did not always understand our needs. We had no money for groceries and he would send us crates of wine! One Christmas, when we had no means to buy a *Weihnachtsbaum* — a Christmas tree — Engels arrived with six bottles of champagne. So, we imagined a tree, formed a circle around it, drank champagne, and sang Christmas songs. *Marx sings, hums a snatch of a Christmas carol:* "Tannenbaum . . ."

I knew what my revolutionary friends were thinking: Marx, the atheist, with a Christmas tree!

Yes, I did describe religion as the opium of the people, but no one has ever paid attention to the full passage. Listen. *He picks up a book and reads:* "Religion is the sigh of the oppressed creature, the heart of a heartless world, the soul of soulless conditions, it is the opium of the people." True, opium is no solution, but it may be necessary to relieve pain. *Shakes his head.* Don't I know that from my boils? And doesn't the world have a terrible case of boils?

I keep thinking about Jenny. *He stops, rubs his eyes.* How she packed all our possessions and brought our two girls, Jennichen and Laura, across the Channel to London. And then gave birth three times in our miserable cold flat on Dean Street. Nursed those babies and tried to keep them warm. And saw them die one by one . . . Guido, he had not even begun to walk. And Francesca, she was one year old . . . I had to borrow three pounds to pay for her coffin . . . As for Moosh, he lived for eight years, but something was wrong from the start. He had a large handsome head, but the rest of him never grew. The night he died, we all slept on the floor around his body until the morning came.

When Eleanor was born, we were fearful. But she was a tough little thing. It was good that she had two older sisters. They had barely survived themselves. Jennichen was born in Paris. Paris is marvelous for lovers, but not for children. Something about the air. Laura was our second, born in Brussels. No one should be born in Brussels.

In London, we had no money. But we always had Sunday picnics. We would walk an hour and a half into the countryside, Jenny and I, the children, and Lenchen (oh, I'll tell you about her . . .). Lenchen would make a roast veal. And we would have tea, fruit bread, cheese, beer. Eleanor was the youngest, but she drank beer.

No money, but children need a vacation. Once, I took the rent money and sent them to the Atlantic coast of France. Another time, with our groceries money, I bought a piano, because the girls loved music.

A father is not supposed to have favorites among his children. But Eleanor! I would say to Jenny: "Eleanor is a strange child." And Jenny would reply: "You expect the children of Karl Marx to be normal?"

Eleanor was the youngest, the brightest. Imagine a revolutionary at the age of eight. That's how old she was in 1863. Poland was in rebellion against Russian rule, and Tussy wrote a letter (that's what we called her: Tussy) — she wrote to Engels about "those brave little fellows in Poland," as she called them. When she was nine, she sent a letter to America, advice to President Lincoln, telling him how to win the war against the Confederacy!

Also, she smoked. And drank wine. Still, she was a child. She would dress her dolls . . . while sipping from a glass of wine! She played chess with me when she was ten, and I could not easily defeat her. At fifteen, she suddenly became furious against the law about observing the Lord's Day. No activity on Sunday was permitted. So, she organized "Sunday Evenings for the People" at St. Martin's Hall, brought musicians there to play Handel, Mozart, Beethoven. The hall was packed. Two thousand people. It was illegal, but no one was arrested. A lesson. If you are going to break the law, do it with two thousand people . . . and Mozart.

I used to read Shakespeare and Aeschylus and Dante aloud to her and her sisters, which she loved. Her room was a Shakespeare museum. She memorized *Romeo and Juliet* and insisted that I read, over and over, those lines of Romeo, when he sees Juliet for the first time:

The brightness of her cheek would shame those stars
As daylight doth a lamp; her eyes in heaven
Would through the airy region stream so bright
That birds would sing and think it were not night.

Tussy was not easy to live with. Oh, no! Do you know how embarrassing it is to have a child who finds flaws in your reasoning? She would argue with me about my writings! For instance, my essay "On the Jewish Question." Not easy to understand, I admit. Well, Eleanor read it, and immediately challenged me: "Why do you single out the Jews as representatives of capitalism? They are not the only ones poisoned by commerce and greed."

I tried to explain: I wasn't singling out the Jews, just using them as a vivid example. Her answer was to start wearing a Jewish star. "I'm a Jew," she announced. What could I say? I shrugged my shoulders and Eleanor said: *"That's a very Jewish gesture."* She could be very annoying!

Tussy knew my father had converted to Christianity. It was not practical to be a Jew in Germany . . . Is it ever practical to be a Jew, anywhere? He had me baptized at the age of eight. This fact intrigued Eleanor. She asked: "Moor" — the family called me Moor because of my dark complexion — "I know you were baptized. But first you were circumcised, weren't you?" Nothing embarrassed that girl!

At such times she was impossible. Listen to this. Alongside her Jewish star, she wore her crucifix. No, she was not enamored of Christianity, but of the Irish, and their rebellion against England. She learned about the Irish struggle from Lizzie Burns, Engels' love.

Lizzie was a mill girl and could not read. Engels spoke nine languages. You might think this would make it hard for them to communicate. But they loved one another. Lizzie was active in the Irish movement. Tussy would visit and the two of them would sit on the floor and drink wine together and sing Irish songs until they fell asleep.

There was that terrible night, the night the English government hanged two young Irishmen, right there in Soho, with a drunken crowd cheering . . . Those genteel English with their afternoon tea and their public hangings! I understand you don't hang people anymore — only gas them, or inject poison into their veins, or use electricity to burn them to death. Much more civilized. Yes, they hanged two young Irishmen for wanting freedom from England. Eleanor wept and wept.

I would say to her: "Tussy, you don't have to get involved so soon with the horrors of the world. You're fifteen." And she would answer: "That's the point, Moor. I'm not thirteen. I'm not fourteen. I'm *fifteen*."

Yes, she was fifteen, and she became infatuated with any dashing, handsome man who visited our flat. I could draw up a list. For all the rest of her life, Eleanor was clever in politics, idiotic in love. She was mad about the hero of the Paris Commune, Lissagaray. Well, at least he was a Frenchman.

Jennichen's fellow was English. English men are like English food. Need I say more? And there was Laura's lover, LaFargue. His public displays of ardor were absurd. He would put his hand on her ass, in public, as if it were the most natural thing. And Jenny defended him. "It's his Creole background," she said. "You know his family came to France from Cuba." As if in Cuba everyone went around with their hands on somebody's ass!

Sighs. Jenny was always trying to calm me down. Well, she might calm *me*, but she was unsuccessful with my boils. *Grimaces.* Did you ever have boils? There is no sickness more odious. They plagued me all my life. And led to stupid attempts to analyze me via my boils. "Marx is angry at the capitalist system because he has boils!" What imbeciles!

How do they account for all the revolutionaries who don't have boils?

Of course, they always find something: this one was beaten by his father; this one was nursed by his mother until he was ten; that one had no toilet training — as if one must be abnormal to resent exploitation. Every explanation except the obvious one, that capitalism, by its nature, its attack on the human spirit, breeds rebellion . . .

Oh yes, they say capitalism has become more humane since my time. Really? Just a few years ago — it was in the newspapers — factory owners locked the doors on the women in their chicken factory in North Carolina. Why? To make more profit. There was a fire, and twenty-five workers were trapped, burned to death.

Perhaps my anger did inflame my boils. But try working, try sitting and writing, with boils on your ass! And don't tell me about doctors. The doctors knew less than I did. Much less, because the boils were mine. *Takes another drink of beer.*

I could not sleep. Then I discovered something miraculous — water. Yes, as simple as that. Cloths soaked in warm water. Jenny would apply them patiently, hour after hour. She would wake up in the middle of the night when I cried out, and apply those soothing wet cloths . . . Sometimes, when Jenny was away, Lenchen would do that.

He stops to reflect. Yes, Lenchen. Here we are, living in poverty in Soho, and Jenny's mother decides to send us Lenchen, to help with the babies. We had pawned our furniture, but suddenly we had a servant girl. That's how it is when you marry into aristocracy. Your in-laws don't send you money, which you desperately need. They send you fine linens and silverware. And a servant. Actually, not a bad idea. The servant can take the linens and silverware to the pawnshop and get some money. Lenchen did that many times . . .

But she was never a servant. The children adored her. And Jenny had tremendous affection for her. When Jenny was ill, Lenchen was with her, tending to every need.

But, yes, her presence created a great tension between Jenny and me. I remember a scene. Jenny said: "This morning, I saw you looking at Lenchen."

"Looking? What do you mean?"

"I mean the way a man looks at a woman."

"I still don't know what you mean." *Shakes his head sadly.* It was one of those conversations which cannot possibly come to any good.

There was all this going on inside our flat on Dean Street. And outside was London . . . Can you imagine the streets of London in 1858? The coster girls, trying to sell a few rolls for a few pennies. The organ grinder with his monkey. The prostitutes, the magicians, the fire-eaters, the street vendors bellowing trumpets, ringing bells, the hurdy-gurdies, the organs, the brass bands, the fiddlers, the Scottish pipers, and always a beggar girl singing an Irish ballad. That's what I saw and heard, walking home every evening from the British Museum, under the gas lamps that had just been lit, until I got to Dean Street and made my way through the mud and sewage, thinking about the care they took in paving streets of the wealthy neighborhoods. *Sighs.* Well, I suppose it was only fitting that the author of *Das Kapital* should slog through shit while writing his condemnation of the capitalist system . . .

Jenny did not sympathize with my complaints about wading through the mud on the street. She would say: "That's how it feels to me reading *Das Kapital!*" She was always my severest critic. Unsparing. Honest, you might say. Is there anything more outrageous than an honest critic?

The book troubled her. Yes, *Das Kapital. Picks up the book.* She worried that I would bore people from the start with my discussion of commodities, use value, exchange value. She said the book was too long, too detailed. She used the word "ponderous." Imagine!

She reminded me what our trade union friend Peter Fox said when I gave him the book. "I feel like a man who has been given an elephant as a gift."

Yes, Jenny said, it *is* an elephant. I tried to tell her this is not the *Communist Manifesto,* which was intended for the general public. It is an analysis.

"Let it be an analysis," she said. "But let it cry out like the *Manifesto.*"

"*A spectre is haunting Europe — the spectre of Communism!* Yes," she said, "that excites the reader . . . *A spectre is haunting Europe!*"

And then she read to me the first words of *Das Kapital,* to torment me, of course. *Marx picks the book from the table, and reads:* "The wealth of those societies in which the capitalist mode of production prevails presents itself as an immense accumulation of commodities."

She said, "That will put readers to sleep."

I ask you, is that boring? *He thinks.* Maybe it is a little boring. I admitted that to Jenny. She said, "There's no such thing as *a little* boring."

Don't misunderstand. She did see *Das Kapital* as a profound analysis. It showed how the capitalist system must, at a certain stage in history, come into being and bring about a colossal growth of the productive forces, an unprecedented increase in the wealth of the world. And then how it must, by its own nature, distribute that wealth in such a way as to destroy the humanity of both laborer and capitalist. And how it must, by its nature, create its own gravediggers and give way to a more human system.

But Jenny always asked, "Are we reaching the people we want to reach?"

One day, she said to me: "Do you know why the censors have allowed it to be published? Because they cannot understand it and assume no one else will."

I reminded her that *Das Kapital* was receiving favorable reviews. She reminded me that most of the reviews were written by Engels ... I told her that perhaps she was being critical of my work because she was unhappy with me.

"You men!" she said. "You cannot believe that your work *deserves* criticism and so you attribute it to something personal. Yes, Moor, my personal feelings are there, but this is separate."

Yes, her personal feelings. Jenny was having a terrible time then. I suppose I was responsible. But I did not know how to ease her anguish. You must understand, Jenny and I fell in love when I was seventeen and she was nineteen. She was marvelous looking, with auburn hair and dark eyes. For some reason, her family took a liking to me. They were aristocrats. Aristocrats are always impressed with intellectuals. Jenny's father and I would have long discussions about Greek philosophy. I had done my doctoral thesis on Democritus and Heraclitus. I was beginning to realize that up to now the philosophers had only interpreted the world. But the point was to *change* it!

When I was expelled from Germany, Jenny followed me to Paris and there we married and she gave birth to Jennichen and Laura. We were happy in Paris, living on nothing, meeting our friends in a café. They also lived on nothing. What a bunch we were! Bakunin, the huge, shaggy anarchist. Engels, the handsome atheist. Heine, the saintly poet. Oh,

Stirner, the total misfit. And Proudhon, who said, "Property is theft!" . . . but wanted some!

Being poor in Paris is one thing. Being poor in London is another. We moved there with two children, and soon Jenny was pregnant again. Sometimes I felt she blamed me for having to bring up our children in a cold, damp flat where someone was sick all the time.

Jenny came down with smallpox. She recovered, but it left pockmarks on her face. I tried to tell her she was still beautiful, but it didn't help.

I wish you could know Jenny. What she did for me cannot be calculated. And she accepted the fact that I could not simply get a job like other men. Yes, I did try once. I wrote a letter of inquiry to the railway for a position as clerk. They responded as follows: "Dr. Marx, we are honored with your request for a position here. We have never had a doctor of philosophy working for us as a clerk. But the position requires a legible handwriting, so we must regretfully decline your offer." *He shrugs.*

Jenny believed in my ideas. But she was impatient with what she considered the pretensions of high-level scholarship. "Come down to earth, Herr Doktor," she would say.

She wanted me to describe the theory of surplus value so ordinary workers could understand it. I told her, "No one can understand it without first understanding the labor theory of value, and how labor power is a special commodity whose value is determined by the cost of the means of subsistence and yet gives value to all other commodities, a value which always exceeds the value of labor power."

She would shake her head: "No, that won't do. All you have to say is this: your employer gives you the barest amount in wages, just enough for you to survive and work; but out of your labor he makes far more than what he pays you. And so he gets richer and richer, while you stay poor."

All right, let us say only a hundred people in world history have ever understood my theory of surplus value. *Gets heated.* But it is still true! Just last week, I was reading the reports of the United States Department of Labor. There you have it. Your workers are producing more and more goods and getting less and less in wages. What is the result? Just as I predicted. Now the richest one percent of the American population owns forty percent of the nation's wealth. And this in the great model of world capitalism, the nation that has not only robbed its own people, but sucked in the wealth of the rest of the world . . .

Jenny was always trying to simplify ideas that were, by their nature, complex. She accused me of being a scholar first and a revolutionary second. She said: "Forget your intellectual readers. Address the workers."

She called me arrogant and intolerant. "Why do you attack other revolutionaries more vehemently than you attack the bourgeoisie?" she asked.

Proudhon, for instance. The man did not understand that we must applaud capitalism for its development of giant industries, and then take them over. Proudhon thought we must retreat into a more simple society. When he wrote his book *The Philosophy of Poverty*, I replied with my own book, *The Poverty of Philosophy*. I thought this was clever. Jenny thought it was insulting. *Sighs.* I suppose Jenny was a far better human being than I could ever be.

She encouraged me to get off my behind and get involved in the cause of the London workers. She came with me when I was invited to address the first meeting of the International Working Men's Association. It was the fall of 1864. Two thousand people were packed into St. Martin's Hall. *Steps forward, ex-*

tends his arm as if to a great crowd as he speaks very deliberately, powerfully:

"The workers of all countries must unite against foreign policies which are criminal, which play upon national prejudices, which squander, in wars, the people's blood and treasure. We must combine across national boundaries to vindicate the simple laws of morals and justice in international affairs . . . Workers of the world, unite!" *Pauses . . .*

Jenny liked that . . . *Takes a drink.*

She kept the family going, with the water cut off, the gas cut off. But she never tired of the subject of female emancipation. She said that the vitality of women was being sapped by staying at home and darning socks and cooking. And so she refused to stay at home.

She accused me of being theoretically an emancipationist but practically ignorant of the problems of women. "You and Engels," she said, "write about sexual equality, but you do not practice it." Well, I won't comment on that . . .

She supported with all her heart the Irish struggle against England. Queen Victoria had said, "These Irish are really abominable people — not like any other civilized nation." Jenny wrote a letter to the London newspapers: "England hangs Irish rebels, who wanted nothing but freedom. Is England a civilized nation?"

Jenny and I were powerfully in love. How can I make you understand that? But we went through hellish times in London. The love was still there. But, at a certain point, things changed. I don't know why. Jenny said it was because she was no longer the great beauty I had wooed. That made me angry. She said it was because of Lenchen. That made me even more angry. She said I was angry because it was true. That made me furious!

He sighs, takes a swallow of beer, looks over the newspapers on the table, picks one up. They claim that because the Soviet Union collapsed, Communism is dead. *Shakes his head.* Do these idiots know what Communism is? Do they think that a system run by a thug who murders his fellow revolutionaries is Communism? *Scheisskopfen!*

Journalists, politicians who say such things — what kind of education did they have? Did they ever read the *Manifesto* that Engels and I wrote when he was twenty-eight years old and I was thirty?

He reaches for a book on the table and reads: "In place of the old bourgeois society, with its classes and class antagonisms, we shall have an association, in which the free development of each is the condition for the free development of all." Do you hear that? An *association!* Do they understand the objective of Communism? Freedom of the individual! To develop himself, herself, as a compassionate human being. Do they think that someone who calls himself a Communist or a socialist and acts like a gangster understands what Communism is?

To shoot those who disagree with you — can that be the Communism that I gave my life for? That monster who took all power for himself in Russia — and who insisted on interpreting my ideas like a religious fanatic — when he was putting his old comrades up against the wall before firing squads, did he allow his citizens to read that letter I wrote to the *New York Tribune* in which I said that capital punishment could not be justified in any society calling itself civilized? . . . *Angry.* Socialism is not supposed to reproduce the stupidities of capitalism!

Here in America, your prisons are crowded. Who is in them? The poor. Some of them have committed violent and terrible crimes. Most of them are burglars, thieves, robbers, sellers of drugs. They believe in free enterprise! They do what the capitalists do, but on a much smaller scale . . .

He picks up another book. Do you know what Engels and I wrote about prisons? "Rather than punishing individuals for their crimes, we should destroy the social conditions which engender crime, and give to each individual the scope which he needs in society in order to develop his life."

Oh, yes, we spoke of a "dictatorship of the proletariat." Not a dictatorship of a *party*, of a central committee, not a dictatorship of one man. No, we spoke of a temporary dictatorship of the working class. The mass of the people would take over the state and govern in the interests of all — until the state itself would become unnecessary and gradually disappear.

Bakunin, of course, disagreed. He said that a state, even a workers' state, if it has an army, police, prisons, will become a tyranny. He loved to argue with me.

Do you know about him? Bakunin, the anarchist? If a novelist invented such a character, you would say the existence of such a person is not possible. To say Bakunin and I did not get along is a great understatement.

Listen to what he said at the time Engels and I were in Brussels, writing the *Manifesto. Marx picks up a document from the table and reads:* "Marx and Engels, especially Marx, are ingrained bourgeois."

We were ingrained bourgeois! Of course, compared to Bakunin, everyone was bourgeois, because Bakunin chose to live like a pig. And if you did not live like a pig, if you had a roof over your head, if you had a piano in your sitting room, if you enjoyed some fresh bread and wine, you were a bourgeois.

I grant the man courage. He was imprisoned, sent to Siberia, escaped, wandered the world trying to foment revolution everywhere. He wanted an anarchist society, but the only anarchism he ever succeeded in establishing was in his head. He tried to start an uprising in Bologna, and almost killed himself with his own revolver. His revolutions failed everywhere, but he was like a man whose failure with women only spurs him on to more.

Did you ever see a photograph of Bakunin? A giant of a man. Bald head, which he covered with a little gray cap. Massive beard. Ferocious expression. He had no teeth — scurvy, the result of his prison diet. He seemed to live not in this world but in some world of his imagination. He was oblivious to money. When he had it, he gave it away; when he didn't have it, he borrowed without any thought of returning it. He had no home, or, you might say, the world was his home. He would arrive at a comrade's house and announce: "I'm here — where do I sleep? And what is there to eat?" In an hour he was more at home than his hosts!

There was that time in Soho. We were having dinner, and Bakunin burst in. Didn't bother to knock. It was his habit to arrive at dinnertime. We were surprised; we thought he was in Italy. Whenever we heard about him, he was in some far-off country organizing a revolution. Well, he almost knocked the door off its hinges, came in, looked around, smiled his toothless smile, and said, "Good evening, comrades." And without waiting for a response, sat down at the table, and began devouring sausage and meat in enormous chunks, stuffing in cheese, too, and glass after glass of brandy.

I said to him: "Mikhail, try the wine, we have plenty of that; brandy is expensive."

He drank some wine, spit it right out. "Absolutely tasteless," he said. "Brandy helps you think more clearly."

He then began his usual performance, preaching, arguing, ordering, shouting, exhorting. I was furious, but it was Jenny who spoke up. "Mikhail," she said, "Stop! You're consuming all the oxygen in the room!" He just roared with laughter and went on.

Bakunin's head was full of anarchist garbage, romantic, utopian nonsense. I wanted to expel him from the International. Jenny thought this ridiculous. Why, she asked, do revolutionary groups with six members always threaten someone with expulsion?

He had a hundred disguises, because the police were looking for him in every country in Europe. When he came to us in London, he was disguised as a priest. At least he thought so. He looked ridiculous!

Well, he was with us a week. Once we stayed up the whole night, drinking and arguing and drinking some more, until neither of us could walk. In fact, I fell asleep in the midst of one Bakunin's perorations. He shook me until I woke up, saying, "I haven't finished my point."

It was that glorious time in the winter of 1871, when the Commune had taken power in Paris . . . Yes, the Paris Commune. Bakunin leaped, with his full bulk, into that revolution. The French understood him. They had a saying: "On the first day of a revolution, Bakunin is a treasure. On the second day, he should be shot."

Do you know about that magnificent episode in human history, the Paris Commune? The story starts with stupidity. I am speaking of Napoleon the Third. Yes, the nephew of Bonaparte.

He was a buffoon, a stage actor smiling to the crowd while sixteen million French peasants lived in blind dark hovels, their children dying of starvation. But because he kept a legislature, because people voted, it was thought they had democracy . . . A common mistake.

Bonaparte wanted glory, so he made the mistake of attacking Bismarck's armies. He was quickly defeated, whereupon the victorious German troops marched into Paris and were greeted by something more devastating than guns — silence. They found the statues of Paris draped in black, an immense, invisible, silent resistance. They did the wise thing. They paraded through the Arc de Triomphe and quickly departed.

And the old French order, the Republic. Liberals, they called themselves. They did not dare come into

35

Paris. They were trembling with fear because, with the Germans gone, Paris was now taken over by the workers, the housewives, the clerks, the intellectuals, the armed citizens. The people of Paris formed not a government, but something more glorious, something governments everywhere fear, a commune, the collective energy of the people. It was the *Commune de Paris!*

People meeting twenty-four hours a day, all over the city, in knots of three and four, making decisions together, while the city was encircled by the French army, threatening to invade at any moment. Paris became the first free city of the world, the first enclave of liberty in a world of tyranny.

I said to Bakunin: "You want to know what I mean by the dictatorship of the proletariat? Look at the Commune of Paris. That is true democracy." Not the democracy of England or America, where elections are circuses, with people voting for one or another guardian of the old order, where whatever candidate wins, the rich go on ruling the country.

The Commune of Paris. It lived only a few months. But it was the first legislative body in history to represent the poor. Its laws were for them. It abolished their debts, postponed their rents, forced

the pawnshops to return their most needed possessions. They refused to take salaries higher than the
workers. They lowered the hours of bakers. And
planned how to give free admission to the theater
for everyone.

The great Courbet himself, whose paintings had
stunned Europe, presided over the federation of artists. They reopened the museums, set up a commis-
sion for the education of women — something
unheard of — education for women. They took ad-
vantage of the latest in science, the lighter-than-air
balloon, and launched one out of Paris to soar over
the countryside, dropping printed papers for the
peasants, with a simple, powerful message, the message that should be dropped to working people everywhere in the world: *Our interests are the same.*

The Commune declared the purpose of the
schools — to teach children to love and respect their
fellow creatures. I have read your endless discussions
of education. Such nonsense! They teach everything
needed to succeed in the capitalist world. But do
they teach the young to struggle for justice?

The Communards understood the importance of
that. They educated not only by their words, but by
their acts. They destroyed the guillotine, that instru-

ment of tyranny, even of revolutionary tyranny. Then, wearing red scarves, carrying a huge red banner, the buildings festooned with sheets of red silk, they gathered around the Vendôme Column, symbol of military power, a huge statue surmounted by the bronze head of Napoleon Bonaparte. A pulley was attached to the head, a capstan turned, and the head crashed to the ground. People climbed on the ruins. A red flag now floated from the pedestal. Now it was the pedestal not of one country but of the human race, and men and women, watching, wept with joy.

Yes, that was the Commune of Paris. The streets were always full, discussions going on everywhere. People shared things. They seemed to smile more often. Kindness ruled. The streets were safe, without police of any kind. Yes, *that* was socialism!

Of course that example, the example of the Commune, could not be allowed. And so the armies of the Republic marched into Paris and commenced a slaughter. The leaders of the Commune were taken to Père Lachaise cemetery, put against the stone wall, and shot. Altogether, thirty thousand were killed.

The Commune was crushed by wolves and swine. But it was the most glorious achievement of our time . . . *Walks, takes some more beer.*

Bakunin and I drank and argued, drank and argued some more. I said to him: "Mikhail, you don't understand the concept of a proletarian state. We cannot shake off the past in one orgasmic moment. We will have to remake a new society with the remnants of the old order. That takes time."

"No," he said. "The people, overthrowing the old order, must immediately live in freedom or they will lose it."

It began to get personal. I was getting impatient and I said, "You are too stupid to understand."

The brandy was having an effect on him, too. He said: "Marx, you are an arrogant son of a bitch, as always. It is you who don't understand. You think the workers will make a revolution based on your theory? They care not a shit for your theory. Their anger will rise spontaneously, and they will make a revolution without your so-called science. The instinct for revolution is in their bellies." He was aroused. "I spit on your theories."

As he said this, he spat on the floor. What a pig! This was too much. I said: "Mikhail, you can spit on my theories, but not on my floor. Clean it immediately."

"There," he said. "I always knew you were a bully."

I said, "I always knew you were a eunuch."

He roared. It sounded like a prehistoric animal. Then he leaped on top of me. You must understand, the man was enormous. We wrestled on the floor, but were too drunk to really hurt one another. After a while, we were so tired that we just lay there, catching our breath. Then Bakunin rose, like a hippopotamus rising out of a river, unbuttoned his trousers, and began to urinate out the window! I could not believe what I was seeing. "What in hell are you doing, Mikhail?"

"What do you think I'm doing? I'm pissing out your window."

"That is disgusting, Mikhail," I said.

"I'm pissing on London. I'm pissing on the whole British Empire."

"No," I said, "You're pissing on my street."

He didn't reply, just buttoned his pants, lay down on the floor, and began to snore. I lay down on the floor myself, and was soon unconscious.

Jenny found us both like that, hours later, when she woke with the dawn. *Stops to take a swallow of beer.*

No, they could not allow the Commune to live. The Commune was dangerous, too inspiring an example for the rest of the world, so they drowned it in blood. It still happens, does it not, that whenever, in some corner of the world, the old order is pushed aside and people begin to experiment with a new way of living — people innocent of ideology, just angry about their lives — it cannot be permitted. And so they go to work — you know who I mean by *they* — sometimes insidiously, covertly, sometimes directly, violently, to destroy it.

Reading in the newspaper. So, they keep saying: "Capitalism has triumphed." Triumphed! Why? Because the stock market has risen to the sky and the stockholders are even wealthier than before? Triumphed? When one-fourth of American children live in poverty, when forty thousand of them die every year before their first birthday?

Reads from the paper: A hundred thousand people lined up before dawn in New York City for two thousand jobs. What will happen to the ninety-eight thousand who are turned away? Is that why you are building more prisons? Yes, capitalism has triumphed. But over whom?

You have technological marvels, you have sent men into the stratosphere, but what of the people left on earth? Why are they so fearful? Why do they turn to drugs, to alcohol, why do they go berserk and kill? *Holds up the newspaper.* Yes, it's in the newspapers.

Your politicians are bloated with pride. The world will now move toward the "free enterprise system," they say.

Has everyone become stupid? Don't they know the *history* of the free enterprise system? When government did nothing for the people and everything for the rich? When your government gave a hundred million acres of land free to the railroads, but looked away as Chinese immigrants and Irish immigrants worked twelve hours a day on those railroads, and died in the heat and the cold. And when workers rebelled and went on strike, the government sent armies to smash them into submission.

Why the hell did I write *Das Kapital* if not because I saw the misery of capitalism, of the "free enterprise system"? In England, little children were put to work in the textile mills because their tiny fingers could work the spindles. In America, young girls went to work in the mills of Massachusetts at the age of ten and died at the age of twenty-five. The cities were cesspools of vice and poverty. That is capitalism, then and now.

Yes, I see the luxuries advertised in your magazines and on your screens. *Sighs.* Yes, all those screens with all those pictures. You see so much and know so little!

Doesn't anyone read history? *He is angry.* What kind of shit do they teach in the schools these days? *Flashing lights, threatening. Looks up.* They are so sensitive!

I miss Jenny. She would have something to say about all this. I watched her die, sick and miserable at the end. But surely she remembered our years of pleasure, our moments of ecstasy, in Paris, even in Soho.

I miss my daughters . . .

Picks up newspaper again, reads: "Anniversary of Gulf War. A victory, short and sweet." Yes, I know about these short, sweet wars, which leave thousands of corpses in the fields and children dying for lack of food and medicine. *Waves the newspaper.* In

Europe, Africa, Palestine, people killing one another over boundaries. *He is anguished.*

Didn't you hear what I said a hundred and fifty years ago? Wipe out these ridiculous national boundaries! No more passports, no more visas, no more border guards or immigration quotas. No more flags and pledges of allegiance to some artificial entity called a nation. Workers of the world, unite! *He clutches his hip, walks around.* Oh, God, my backside is killing me . . .

I confess: I did not reckon with capitalism's ingeniousness in surviving. I did not imagine that there would be drugs to keep the sick system alive. War to keep the industries going, to make people crazed with patriotism so they would forget their misery. Religious fanatics promising the masses that Jesus will return. *Shakes his head.* I know Jesus. He's not coming back . . .

I was wrong in 1848, thinking capitalism was on its way out. My timing was a bit off. Perhaps by two hundred years. *Smiles.* But it will be transformed. All the present systems will be transformed. People are not fools. I remember your President Lincoln saying that you can't fool all of the people all of the time.

Their common sense, their instinct for decency and justice, will bring them together.

Don't scoff! It has happened before. It can happen again, on a much larger scale. And when it does, the rulers of society, with all their wealth, with all their armies, will be helpless to prevent it. Their servants will refuse to serve, their soldiers will disobey orders.

Yes, capitalism has accomplished wonders unsurpassed in history — miracles of technology and science. But it is preparing its own death. Its voracious appetite for profit — more, more, more! — creates a world of turmoil. It turns everything — art, literature, music, beauty itself — into commodities to be bought and sold. It turns human beings into commodities. Not just the factory worker, but the physician, the scientist, the lawyer, the poet, the artists — all must sell themselves to survive.

And what will happen when all these people realize that they are all workers, that they have a common enemy? They will join with others in order to fulfill themselves. And not just in their own country, because capitalism needs a world market. Its cry is "Free trade!" because it needs to roam freely everywhere in the globe to make more profit — more,

more! But in doing so, it creates, unwittingly, a world culture. People cross borders as never before in history. Ideas cross borders. Something new is bound to come of this. *Pauses, contemplatively.*

When I was in Paris with Jenny in 1843, I was twenty-five, and I wrote that in the new industrial system people are estranged from their work because it is distasteful to them. They are estranged from nature, as machines, smoke, smells, noise invade their senses — progress, it is called. They are estranged from others because everyone is set against everyone else, scrambling for survival. And they are estranged from their own selves, living lives that are not their own, living as they do not really want to live, so that a good life is possible only in dreams, in fantasy.

But it does not have to be. There is still a possibility of choice. Only a possibility, I grant. Nothing is certain. That is now clear. I was too damned certain. Now I know — anything can happen. But people must get off their asses!

Does that sound too radical for you? Remember, to be radical is simply to grasp the root of a problem. And the root is *us*.

I have a suggestion. Pretend you have boils. Pretend that sitting on your ass gives you enormous pain, so you must stand up. You must move, must act.

Let's not speak anymore about capitalism, socialism. Let's just speak of using the incredible wealth of the earth for human beings. Give people what they need: food, medicine, clean air, pure water, trees and grass, pleasant homes to live in, some hours of work, more hours of leisure. Don't ask who deserves it. Every human being deserves it.

Well, it's time to go.

Picks up his belongings. Starts to go, turns.

Do you resent my coming back and irritating you? Look at it this way. It is the second coming. Christ couldn't make it, so Marx came . . .

a short
annotated
reading list

Marx's *Das Kapital* (available in many editions) is, of course, the quintessential Marxian work on political economy. No need to read volumes two and three, unless you are in for a long prison term. Or the *Grundrisse*, which he wrote before he got to the three volumes. Or the three volumes on *Theories of Surplus Value*, which will kill you.

The Eighteenth Brumaire of Louis Bonaparte, on the events in France following the revolution of 1848, is probably the most brilliant, stylistically, of Marx's works.

The *Communist Manifesto,* of course, is short and salty.

For an excellent anthology of works by Marx and Engels, see Robert C. Tucker, *The Marx-Engels Reader*, published by W.W. Norton in New York.

The most useful biography for me, because it deals not just with Marx's life but with his writings, is by the English writer David McLellan: *Karl Marx: His Life and Thought*, published by Harper and Row in New York.

Indispensable for understanding Marx's family life is the two-volume biography of his youngest daughter, Eleanor, by Yvonne Kapp: *Eleanor Marx*, published by Pantheon Books, New York.

There is an interesting biography of Marx's extraordinary wife by H.F. Peters, *Red Jenny*, published by St. Martin's Press in New York.

For a remarkable picture of the London in which Marx and his family lived, see Henry Mayhew's *London Labour and the London Poor*, originally in four volumes, but compressed into one volume by Penguin Books.

a note on
marx in soho

Marx in Soho was first performed in 1995 at the Church Street Theater in Washington, D.C. In 1996, it was performed at Carleton College and Mankato State University in Minnesota. The Broadway Arts Center in Asheville, North Carolina, staged *Marx in Soho* in 1997. The play was also read in 1998 at Boston University in Massachusetts.

To obtain permission for creative performances of *Marx in Soho,* please write to Howard Zinn, South End Press, 7 Brookline Street, Suite 1, Cambridge, MA 02139-4146.

index

index

Books by Howard Zinn available from Haymarket Books

Disobedience and Democracy
Nine Fallacies on Law and Order

❧

Failure to Quit
Reflections of an Optimistic Historian

❧

Vietnam
The Logic of Withdrawal

❧

SNCC
The New Abolitionists

❧

The Southern Mystique

❧

Justice in Everyday Life
The Way It Really Works

❧

Postwar America
1945–1971

❧

Emma
A Play in Two Acts About Emma Goldman, American Anarchist

❧

Marx in Soho
A Play on History

order online from HaymarketBooks.org